FOOD

PETER D. RILEY

Heinemann
LIBRARY

First published in Great Britain by Heinemann Library
Halley Court, Jordan Hill, Oxford OX2 8EJ
a division of Reed Educational and Professional Publishing Ltd.
Heinemann is a registered trademark of Reed Educational &
Professional Publishing Limited.

OXFORD FLORENCE PRAGUE MADRID ATHENS
MELBOURNE AUCKLAND KUALA LUMPUR SINGAPORE TOKYO
IBADAN NAIROBI KAMPALA JOHANNESBURG GABORONE
PORTSMOUTH NH CHICAGO MEXICO CITY SAO PAULO

Designed by Visual Image
Printed in Hong Kong

02 01 00 99 98
10 9 8 7 6 5 4 3 2 1

ISBN 0 431 08436 X

British Library Cataloguing in Publication Data

Riley, Peter, 1947-
   Food – (Cycles in science)
   1.Nutrition - Juvenile literature 2.Food chains (Ecology) -
   Juvenile literature
   I.Title
   572.4

Acknowledgements
The Publishers would like to thank the following for
permission to reproduce photographs:
Britstock-IFA: Goedel p5; Bruce Coleman Ltd: G
McCarthy p11, J Shaw pp14, 22; Planet Earth
Pictures: J Mackinnon p8, J R Bracegirdle p9, S
Hopkin p10, F Kristo p16, E Beaton p17, Paulo de
Oliveira p27; SPL: J Durham p6, J Hinsch p7, D
Nunnuk p13, M Dohsu p19, C Nuridsany & M
Perennou p25, J Holmes & Cell Tech Ltd p28, P
Melzel p29; Tony Stone Images: Frans Lanting p4, S
Lowry p12, Manoj Shah p15, M Rosenfeld p18, A
Brando p20, K Lamm p23, C Keeler p24, B Baunton
p26; Zefa: T Stewart p21.

Cover photograph reproduced with permission of Dr
Jeremy Burgess, Science Photo Library

Our thanks to Jim Drake for his comments in the
preparation of this book.

Every effort has been made to contact copyright
holders of any material reproduced in this book. Any
omissions will be rectified in subsequent printings if
notice is given to the Publisher.

Any words appearing in the text in bold, **like
this**, are explained in the Glossary.

CONTENTS

FOOD

The energy that drives the food cycle does not come from the Earth. It comes from 150 million kilometres away. It is generated in a natural nuclear reactor more than a million times the size of the Earth – the Sun. If the Earth were nearer the Sun it would be too hot for life and if it were further away it would be too cold. The amount of heat and light energy reaching the Earth is just right for living things to survive.

WHY FOOD IS IMPORTANT

Food contains energy from the Sun and materials from the Earth. They are brought together in green plants in a process called **photosynthesis**. The energy in food is used to power the life processes in living things. The materials in food form chemicals called nutrients. Nutrients are used by all living things to build their bodies and keep them healthy.

Tropical rainforests grow in hot, damp regions of the world. These conditions allow the plants to grow well and produce a good quantity of food for the animals, such as these parrots.

WHO'S WHO IN THE FOOD CYCLE

Only green plants can make food on the Earth's surface. Animals must get their food second hand, by eating plants or other animals. Many **micro-organisms** get their food from the dead bodies of plants and animals as they decay.

The path of food, from plant to animal to micro-organism, forms the major part of the food cycle. Humans are a part of the food cycle too. We can live for up to only six weeks without food and need certain amounts of different foods each day to get the right nutrients to keep healthy.

This food provides the cyclists with energy to continue their journey. It helps the younger members of the party grow and provides everyone with materials to repair their cuts and bruises if they fall off their bicycles.

HUMAN SURVIVAL IN THE FOOD CYCLE

The first people hunted animals and collected fruit and roots to eat. Later, people learnt how to grow crops and how to keep animals. They were better fed, they lived longer and had more children. Slowly the human population increased.

Today, the human population on Earth is so large that vast areas of land have to be used to produce our food. The food cycles of other living things have been destroyed or put at risk in order to provide enough food for humans. In some instances our own place in the food cycle has been affected. However, many people today still do not receive enough food to keep them healthy.

THE FOOD CYCLE BEGINS

The first investigations into how a food cycle begins were made 400 years ago. Since then many more observations and experiments have been made and we now know how food is made – from sunlight, air and water.

A LONG EXPERIMENT

In the 17th century Jan Baptiste van Helmont, a doctor born in Brussels, performed an experiment on a young willow tree to find out where its food came from. He weighed out some soil and put it in a pot. Then he weighed the young tree and planted it in the soil. He watered the soil regularly but added nothing else. After five years he dug up the tree and weighed it and he weighed the soil too. He was amazed to find that the **mass** of the tree had increased over 74 kilograms but the mass of the soil had decreased less than 6 grams. He concluded that the soil could not have provided much of the new material and thought that most of it must have been provided by the water. Later experiments by others showed that he was only partly right, because plants also use air and sunlight to grow.

Inside these microscopic leaf cells you can see green discs called chloroplasts which trap sunlight.

IN THE FOOD FACTORY

What nobody knew in van Helmont's time was that water passes up inside the plant from the root to the leaf in **microscopic** pipes. On the underside of many leaves are microscopic holes.

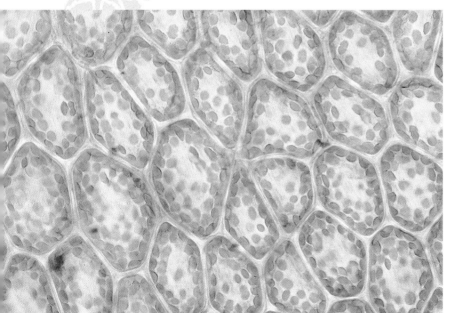

Carbon dioxide gas from the air goes through these holes into the leaf. It takes part in a chemical reaction with the water to make **carbohydrates** – one of the important groups of nutrients. The energy to make this change comes from the sunlight trapped by the green pigment called **chlorophyll**. As light is used to build up food the process is called **photosynthesis** from the Greek words 'photo' meaning light and 'synthesis' meaning build up.

The bodies of diatoms are grouped together in this drop of sea water.

CELLS

The bodies of most living things are made from cells. Cells are like tiny boxes or packets about one-fiftieth of a millimetre across. In green plants the leaf cells contain green discs called chloroplasts. They contain the chlorophyll.

Some plants called diatoms have bodies made out of just one cell. They are found in huge numbers in the surface of the sea where they form part of the **plankton**. Their tiny bodies form food for the animals in the plankton.

ANIMALS

The food cycle continues as animals feed. Most animals must break down the bodies of other living things to get the food they need. Each kind of animal feeds on certain types of food and would starve if they were given anything else. For example, a rabbit does not eat meat and a dog does not make a meal of cabbage leaves. A few animals are able to feed on a wide range of foods, which may come from both plants and other animals.

BREAKING DOWN THE FOOD

Almost all animals have a digestive system. This is a tube which runs through the animal's body. As food is eaten it passes into this tube and is broken down. If the food is large, like a leaf or a piece of meat, it is broken down in stages. First, it is broken down into small particles and then **nutrients** that can pass into the blood. For example, the protein found in meat or beans is broken down into **amino acids**. They travel in the blood to all parts of the body and are used for growth, maintenance and the repair of damaged parts, such as cuts and bruises on the skin.

THE PLANT EATERS

Roe deer eat a wide range of leaves and are typical herbivores.

Animals that feed on plants are called herbivores. Almost every part of a plant is eaten by some kind of herbivore. Roundworms may feed among the roots.

Above ground, a caterpillar may go unnoticed as it eats its way around a leaf. A monkey may eat the fruit in the tree tops while an elephant may rip off the bark of a tree with its tusks.

This lioness finishing her meal of meat is an example of a carnivore.

THE ANIMAL EATERS

Animals which feed on other animals are called carnivores. A spider eating a fly is a carnivore and so is a frog eating a slug. Carnivores use a variety of ways to get a meal. A cheetah uses speed to run down a gazelle while a pride of lions may work as a team to spring an ambush on a zebra. Snakes and spiders may use poison to stop their prey struggling.

A MORE VARIED DIET

Some animals eat both plants and animals. These animals are called omnivores. Two examples of omnivores are the wild pig and the bear. Wild pigs eat roots, bulbs, grubs and earthworms while bears eat fish, berries and honey. Most humans are omnivores too.

DEAD BODIES

What happens to the bodies of plants and animals when they die? For centuries people had conflicting theories about this. When dead bodies were observed closely by anatomists in the 17th century they found living things feeding on them.

EATING DEAD BODIES

The bodies of animals are torn apart and eaten by scavengers. These are animals which eat a wide range of foods. For example a crow will eat berries, seeds, insects and frogs but will also feed on any animal that has been killed. Vultures are one of the best known scavengers although they also hunt rodents, flamingo chicks and fish. Vultures have wide broad wings for gliding over long distances to search for dead elephants or an animal killed by a lion on the African plains.

ROTTING AND REBIRTH

Many people used to believe that when something rotted away it changed into another living thing. For example, they thought that when grain went mouldy it turned into mice, and that rotting meat turned into maggots.

This fly is laying eggs in rotting meat. Maggots will hatch from the eggs and feed on the meat. Later each maggot will change into a pupa then change again into a fly.

In 1668 Francesco Redi, an Italian doctor, tested this idea with a dead snake, some fish and meat. He divided them up into open and closed flasks. He saw that flies visited the flesh in the open flasks but they could not reach the flesh in the closed flasks. Later maggots emerged from the flesh in the open flasks but none emerged from the flesh in the closed flasks. The theory of rotting and rebirth was disproved.

A FEAST FOR FUNGUS

A fungus is a kind of plant that does not have **chlorophyll**. It cannot use the energy in sunlight to make its own food and feeds on the bodies of other living things. When a fungus is fully grown it produces **spores** and releases them into the air. These are so small that they can only be seen under a microscope. A spore is similar to a seed but when it grows it does not form roots but forms thin threads which digest dead plants and animals. The threads branch out to form a network as the fungus feeds.

The fungus feeding inside this dead tree has sent out fruiting bodies to release spores into the air.

RECYCLING

*When scavengers and fungi have finished feeding, the remains of the dead plants and animals are left. These become the food of **micro-organisms**, as do the wastes of animals. After the micro-organisms have finished feeding nothing is left but **raw materials**, the building blocks of living things. These are returned back to the soil. Animals, including humans, do their share of recycling too.*

MICRO-ORGANISMS AND MINERALS

Bacteria are the main kind of micro-organism that recycle materials in the soil. A single bacterium may be one hundredth of a millimetre long. A gram of soil may contain up to 3000 million bacteria. They feed by digesting the remains of dead plants and animals in the soil. They also feed on animal droppings and wastes.

As bacteria feed they change most of their food back into the raw materials from which it was formed. The raw materials are mainly substances called **minerals**. These minerals dissolve in the soil water and are taken up by plant roots. A plant uses them to make cell parts and to drive its life processes. The minerals pass into a herbivore's body when it feeds on the plant. When a carnivore eats a herbivore, the minerals pass into the carnivore's body. Eventually, when the carnivore dies, bacteria feed on its body and release the minerals which can be used as raw materials once again. There would be no breakdown of dead bodies and wastes without bacteria. Imagine the world without them!

These bacteria are the last living things to feed on the remains of plants and animals.

WHY CARBON DIOXIDE IS IMPORTANT

Carbon dioxide goes round and round the food cycle.

Plants make **carbohydrates** by **photosynthesis** (see page 7). They make them because they are a way of storing energy. The plants (and animals that eat them) need this energy to stay alive and grow. When animals take the energy from carbohydrates, carbon dioxide is released. They cannot use the carbon dioxide so they breathe it out. Bacteria also release carbon dioxide into the air when they break down dead plants and animals. The carbon dioxide in the air is recycled because plants take it in while photosynthesizing, to make more carbohydrates! And so the cycle goes on.

The minerals in this manure will be released by bacteria in the soil and taken up by crop plants to make food for you to eat.

HOW OXYGEN IS VITAL

Most living things **respire** using oxygen. They cannot get the energy from their food without it. If there is a lack of oxygen most living things die. In respiration the oxygen is used up but when photosynthesis takes place oxygen is released into the air. This oxygen is free to be used by living things once again to release energy from their food.

FOOD WEBS

*Plants and animals live together in places called habitats. The pathway of the **food cycle** through a habitat can be found by finding out the food of each animal. The way plants and animals are linked together through feeding is called a food chain. There are often many food chains in a habitat and they are linked together into a **food web**.*

This shows one link in the food chain of a Canadian river. The salmon is eaten by the bear.

A LONG FOOD CHAIN

Nearly all food chains start with energy from sunlight. It is trapped in a plant when the plant makes food. The food passes to a herbivore, then a carnivore and perhaps one or more other carnivores too. For example, in the polar seas the plants in the **plankton** are eaten by tiny shrimp-like animals which are then eaten by smaller fish. The food chain continues with the smaller fish being eaten by larger fish, and the larger fish being eaten by a seal. Finally, the seal may be eaten by a killer whale.

THE NUMBERS COUNT

The numbers of living things at each link in the food chain follow a trend. There is usually a very large number of plants, a small number of herbivores and an even smaller number of carnivores. To see why the numbers count, imagine what would happen if there were more rabbits than grass.

The rabbits would soon eat all the food and then starve. There must always be much more of the food than the feeder, so the food plant or food animal can breed and replace those that have been eaten.

ON SAFARI

The African plains are rich in a wide range of animal life. The food chains are linked together in a web. Zebra and gazelle feed on grass, lions feed on zebra and gazelle, eagles feed on gazelle, rats and baboons. If the number of one animal changes, the numbers of the others are affected. For example, if the number of gazelles was reduced by people hunting them, then the lions would have to eat more zebras and the eagle would have to eat more rats and baboons.

A small sample of a food web on the African plains. The zebra eat the grass. The lioness eats the zebra.

CHANGES

The number of living things in each link of a food chain is constantly changing. Numbers increase when seedlings take root or young are hatched or born and decrease when herbivores rip up a plant or carnivores make a kill. Sometimes a new plant or animal enters an environment. When this happens it can be disastrous for the other plants and animals living there.

THE BALANCE OF NATURE

Living things breed to replace those of their kind that die. Few animals die of old age as most are eaten by **predators**. Usually the number of **offspring** produced in a year matches the number that die.

The Tasmanian devil was once found over a large area of Australia. It is a hunter and will attack anything from a lizard to a wallaby. Today it is only found in Tasmania.

UPSETTING THE BALANCE NATURALLY

Severe weather in the breeding season can kill many young offspring. There are not enough individuals to replace those that die in the year. The number of a particular animal may fall. Predators of the animal may starve or eat more of other animals to stay alive.

UPSETTING THE BALANCE UNNATURALLY

If a new plant or animal is introduced into a habitat it may greatly increase in number because food may be easy to find and it may have no natural predator. In Australia in 1935 sugar cane farmers wanted to control the number of cane beetle which feed on sugar cane. They introduced the cane toad from Central and South America. The toads were released and they ate lizards, frogs and mice as well as the cane beetle, and their number increased as they had no natural predator in Australia. They have become pests themselves.

The greatest threat to the balance of nature comes from the increasing human population. As more space is needed for farms and cities, habitats are destroyed and plants and animals killed.

The dingo is not native to Australia but was introduced by travellers a few thousand years ago. It will catch and eat a wide range of animals including the kangaroo. As its numbers increased the numbers of the Tasmanian devil decreased and some people think the two changes are related.

YOU AND FOOD

*Your food comes from many places in the world. You are part of many food chains which form a web around the planet. You have to eat a range of foods to get all the **nutrients** you need. Humans are not at the end of their food chains. There are other animals and even a plant that will feed on us if given the chance.*

YOU AND YOUR FOOD CHAINS

There are at least two food chains in a breakfast bowl of **cereal**. One of them is from the cereal to you, and the other starts with grass, which is eaten by the cow that produces the milk that you then drink. The cereal may have been grown thousands of kilometres away in another part of the world while the milk may have come from a farm much closer to your home. In the course of a day you are a link in many food chains. Try to work them out as you eat your meals.

Foods are tested in laboratories to find out the nutrients they contain. This information can be used in planning balanced diets.

THE NUTRIENTS IN YOUR FOOD

The nutrients you need are **carbohydrates** for instant energy; fats for stored energy and to keep you warm; protein for the growth and repair of injured body parts and vitamins and **minerals** for health.

Each food contains one or more nutrients. No single food contains them all. This means that you have to eat a number of different foods.

You can get these nutrients by eating the correct amounts of a wide range of foods. People who do this are said to have a balanced diet. If your meals tend to have a small range of foods, such as beans and chips with little or no fruit, then your diet is not balanced and your health may suffer.

YOU ARE ON THE MENU

Mosquitoes have a mouth like a hollow needle. Male mosquitoes use it to feed on nectar and water. Some types of female mosquito feed on human blood. A **micro-organism** lives inside some mosquitoes and may pass into the human body as it feeds. The micro-organism then feeds and breeds inside the body and causes **malaria**.

If you do not dry between your toes after a bath or shower you may be attacked by a fungus. The fungus feeds on the wet skin and causes the disease called athlete's foot.

This mosquito is feeding on blood. In the blood are the digested foods from the victim's last meal. This provides valuable nutrients for the mosquito.

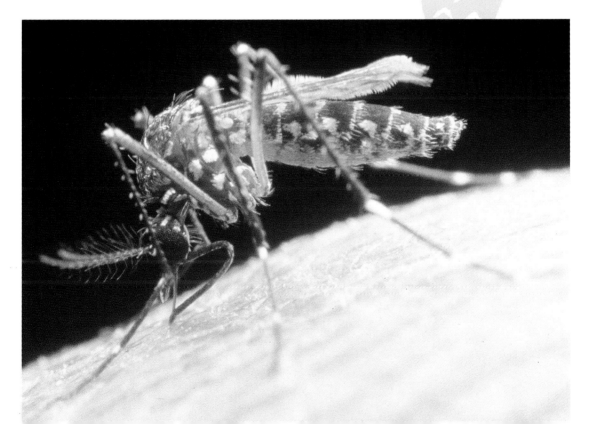

HUNTING THE HIGH SEAS

Fishing is a kind of hunting. People have fished from the earliest times. Today fish are the only type of common food that is still hunted – the rest are farmed. The way fish are caught has changed greatly in the last 60 years but in many places there are fewer fish to catch. Some fish are being farmed now to make sure that there is a constant supply for people to eat.

This is a shoal of jack mackerel. Such fish had a much better chance of escaping from fishermen of the past than they have of getting away from fishermen of today.

FISHING PAST...

In the past, fishing boats were small. They had heavy nets made of rope that fish could see and avoid. The nets were small so the people on board could pull them in as the boats did not have machines to help. Once the fish were on board there was no way of preserving them so the boat had to return to shore so that the catch was still fresh.

By fishing in this way, the catch was small and a huge number of fish remained in the sea. The fish that were left were able to breed and replace the numbers caught.

... AND PRESENT

Now fishing boats are large. They have lightweight nets made of plastic threads which are more difficult for the fish to see and avoid. The boats have powerful machines on board to handle the nets so the nets are much larger than before. The fish can be frozen on board and preserved. This allows the boat to stay at sea for longer as the crew search for more fish.

In many places, the fish that are left cannot breed fast enough to replace those that are caught.

The fish caught in the nets are sorted out on the deck of the fishing boat.

FARMING FISH

At a fish farm the fish are raised from eggs. As they grow they are put in larger and larger ponds. They are fed on **pelleted** food which is thrown into the ponds every day. Salmon, trout, carp and catfish are reared in this way.

FARMING

Humans were not the first farmers. People only began farming about 10,000 years ago. Farming involves caring for living things so that they can be used as food. The soil must be prepared for growing crops which must be planted in a way that will produce the most amount of food. In the past, farm animals were kept outside but now more are being reared inside to supply more meat and eggs.

FARMER ANTS

The first farmers on the planet were ants. Leaf-cutter ants farm a kind of leaf **mould**. They prepare tiny piles of chewed-up leaves in their nests. Fungi **spores** settle on the leaves. Moulds grow from the spores. The ants eat parts of the mould as it grows on the leaves. Some ants farm greenfly in their ant nests. The greenfly produce a sugary liquid called honeydew as they feed. The ants collect the honeydew and feed it to their young.

This land is divided up into fields for growing crops. The fields are larger than where land is used for keeping animals. The trees and bushes with their wildlife have been destroyed.

FARMING CROPS

Most crops grow well in a soil where the rock particles are bound together to make crumbs. **Humus** is the substance which binds the particles. It is formed from the remains of plants. There are large air spaces between the crumbs. They supply oxygen to the **bacteria** feeding on the plant remains and releasing **minerals** into the soil. The large spaces also let water drain through the soil and stop the ground becoming water logged and damaging the crop.

Seeds are sown at intervals along rows that are wide apart. This gives the crop plants space for their roots to grow and collect water, and space for their leaves to catch as much sunlight as possible to make food.

These hens are free to roam outside. If they were kept inside, each hen would be in a cage. Open this book so its covers are at a right angle to see how big the cage would be.

FARMING ANIMALS

Cattle and sheep are kept in fields where they eat grass. The farmer takes care that poisonous plants do not grow with the grass in the fields. The animals are also checked regularly for signs of disease and treated if necessary, to keep them healthy.

Most pigs, turkeys and chickens are reared indoors. The animals do not have the space to roam, so more of the energy in their food is used to build up their bodies. As a result they grow faster and require less food than animals reared outside with more space. Some people say that it is inhumane to keep animals in these conditions but others say it is the only way of meeting the huge demand for cheap meat.

ATTACKS ON OUR FOOD

Crop plants are under attack from other living things. This reduces the amount of food they produce. The attacks can be prevented by the use of poisons. However, some of the poisons contaminate the environment.

These insect pests are attacking the veins of a plant. This will damage the plant and prevent it from growing.

CORNFIELD CRISIS

Weeds, fungi and insects can reduce the size of a crop in a cornfield. Weeds send out roots which compete with the roots of the corn plants and steal some of their water and **minerals**. The weed leaves shade the corn plants and rob them of sunlight. This slows down **photosynthesis** and so the corn grows slowly. Mildew is a fungus which grows on corn plants and rots them.

Insects may nibble away at any part of the plant above or below the soil.

PESTICIDES TO THE RESCUE

Weeds, fungi and insects which damage crops are pests. Chemicals called pesticides have been developed to destroy them. There are three kinds of pesticide: herbicides destroy weeds but leave the crop undamaged; fungicides may be sprayed onto a crop to kill fungi such as mildew; and insecticides may be used to kill insects. A whole crop may be harvested with careful use of pesticides.

THE PROBLEM WITH DDT

DDT is an insecticide that has been used in large amounts. Not all of the pests died when it was used. The ones that survived produced **offspring** that were resistant to the poison. Larger quantities of DDT were used to attack the more resistant insects.

Later it was discovered that DDT did not break down quickly but stayed in the environment and was harmful to living things. For example, if DDT enters lake water it is taken up by the **algae** in the **plankton**. Fish feed on the algae and take in the DDT too. They store it in their body fat. Grebes are birds that feed on fish. If a grebe eats a large number of fish contaminated with DDT it receives so much poison that it dies. Today DDT is banned in many places and alternative insecticides are used. Many of these insecticides break up in the environment after they have done their job and do not contaminate other forms of life.

Pesticides are carefully measured out before spraying to reduce the chances of contaminating the environment.

CYCLE CLASH

The water cycle began 4500 million years ago when the newly formed planet Earth began cooling down. Steam rushed though the cracks in the Earth's surface and condensed to form clouds. They cooled and rained on the rocky surface. The water splashed and gurgled down ravines and settled in huge hollows to make lakes and seas. Some of the water evaporated again to make clouds. This cycle continues to this day. Some of the water that soaks you next time you are caught in a shower may have drenched a dinosaur.

If a small amount of waste enters a river, it is diluted and micro-organisms break it down into nutrients and raw materials. Other living things are not badly affected.

WASTES IN THE WATER

About 1000 million years after the start of the water cycle, the **food cycle** began. As living things grew in numbers and got larger, the amount of wastes they produced got larger too. These wastes formed food for **bacteria**. Later when humans gathered and formed towns, the amount of wastes was too much for the bacteria. The wastes were washed away into rivers which stank with the sewage and harmful bacteria that caused disease.

In 1914 a sewage works opened in Manchester, England which used micro-organisms to treat the wastes. The sewage was sprinkled onto a bed of broken rocks which acted like a filter. As the sewage dripped between the rocks, oxygen in the air and micro-organisms on the rock surfaces destroyed the harmful bacteria. Oxygen and micro-organisms are still used today to treat sewage. In many places the sewage works are not large enough for the towns and cities they serve, so river and sea water is still being polluted.

TOO MUCH FERTILISER

The food cycle crashed into the water cycle yet again in the 20th century. This time it was fertilisers. They were put onto farms in large amounts and when it rained some of the fertiliser was washed into rivers. They caused the growth of many more water plants. When the plants died so much bacteria bred to break them up that they took all the oxygen out of the water. As a result fish and other water life suffocated. Today greater care is taken in controlling the amount of fertiliser used on farms.

If too much waste is poured into a river it cannot be diluted quickly enough. The waste will pollute the water and may kill the plants and animals in the river.

THE FUTURE

As the human population continues to grow, the demand for land constantly increases. This may lead to many changes on our planet. In order to avoid these changes, crop plants and farm animals have been bred to produce more food. Genetic engineering is also being used to increase production further. Biotechnology offers ways of producing food without increasing the need for more land.

THE RAINFOREST PROBLEM

As land is cleared for farms the habitats of plants and animals that live in them are destroyed. A major habitat under threat is the tropical rainforest. The rainforest contains a vast number of different kinds of plants and animals. It has been found that some rainforest plants, such as the tomato, have become useful foods while others are used to make medicines to cure the sick. For example, one kind of tree provides quinine, which is used to reduce fever. If the rainforests are lost the chance to develop some new foods and medicines will be lost too.

This example of genetic engineering shows the different varieties of corn that can be produced by experimenting with the genes from just one variety.

IMPROVING CROPS AND LIVESTOCK

One way to save on space for farming is to make the crops and livestock produce more food. In the past this has been done by making new strains of crop plant or a new breed of farm animal.

For example, a new **cereal** strain is made by selecting plants which produce the most grain on their stalks and breeding them together. The **offspring** of these plants then all produce more grain.

MAKING NEW LIVING THINGS

Every living thing contains instructions in its body that make it grow and live in a particular way. These instructions are called **genes**. Today it is possible to take genes from one living thing and put them in another. This process is called genetic engineering. Here is one example of how genetic engineering could be useful in the **food cycle**. Bean plants have swellings in their roots which become the home of **bacteria** that make fertiliser from nitrogen – a gas in the air. If this feature of a bean could be engineered into other crop plants they could make their own fertiliser. Genetic engineers have to make many checks on their work to avoid producing a living thing that may be harmful.

Inside this fermenter micro-organisms are making food that we can eat.

FOOD FROM A MOULD

Biotechnology is concerned with making new substances from living things. Food called single-cell protein is made by growing **micro-organisms** in large containers called fermenters. One container can produce large amounts of food in a small space.

FOOD FOR EVERYONE

By using the new scientific discoveries wisely, parts of the rainforest and other habitats may yet be saved and enough food could be made for everyone to have a healthy diet.

GLOSSARY

algae (or one alga) green plants without roots, stems or leaves

amino acids a chemical which the body uses for growth and repair

bacteria (or one bacterium) a group of micro-organisms; many feed on the remains of plants and animals, some cause disease

biotechnology an industrial process for making new substances from living things

carbohydrate a chemical substance which provides the body with energy

carbon dioxide a gas released into the air when animals breathe out; it is used by plants to make food

cereal a type of grass plant grown by humans to produce large seeds for food

chlorophyll a green substance found in plants which traps energy in sunlight

condense to change from a gas or vapour into a liquid

evaporate to change from a liquid into a gas or vapour

food cycle the circular path taken by substances used to make food as they move from soil and air to plant and animals and micro-organisms

food web a network made by linking food chains together

gene a chemical instruction which is inherited by the body and makes the body grow or behave in a certain way

genetic engineering a way of moving genes from one type of living thing to another

greenhouse effect the raising of the temperature of the atmosphere by gases such as carbon dioxide which prevent heat from the Sun being reflected from the Earth into space

humus a substance in the soil made from the remains of plants and animals

malaria a disease carried by some mosquitoes which produces a fever that can be fatal

mass the amount of matter or material in a substance

micro-organism a tiny living thing that can only be seen by using a microscope

microscopic so small that it can only be seen by using a microscope

mineral a chemical in the soil which is needed by all living things to keep healthy

mould a growth made by certain types of fungi as they feed on the remains of plants and animals

nucleus the control centre of a cell

nutrient a chemical that is needed by plants and animals to keep them alive and healthy

offspring the young of an animal or plant

pellet a small piece of a substance which has been made into a special shape

photosynthesis the making of carbohydrate food and oxygen by plants using water, carbon dioxide and energy from sunlight

plankton the vast collection of microscopic plants and animals that live in the surface waters of seas and lakes

predator an animal that preys on other animals

ravine a deep narrow valley with steep sides

raw material a material that is used to make another material

respire releasing energy from food for use in life processes

spore a microscopic structure made by fungi and bacteria to reproduce and spread through the air

INDEX